THE DYING PROCESS

A HOSPICE SOCIAL WORKER'S
PERSPECTIVE

ON END OF LIFE CARE

A helpful guide for coping and closure
during end of life care.

Dana Plish, BSW, MA

The Dying Process – A Hospice Social
Worker's Perspective on End of Life Care ©
2014 by Dana Plish.

Kindle Direct Publishing, 2014 eBook

ASIN: B00JTI8XZS

Createspace.com 2014 Print

ISBN 13: 978-1499259834

ISBN 10: 1499259832

Library of Congress Registration Number: TX 7-920-382

Table of Contents

Dedication

I would like to dedicate this book to the memory of my father-in-law, Carl D. Skidmore. I wanted to express my admiration for your courage and grace as you faced death. It is my hope that the memory of your passing will encourage me to always treat others with love and compassion. I also want to thank my parents for their openness and honesty and their lifetime of love and support. I want to thank them for instilling in me the desire to treat all people with love and respect. Thank you, Dad for helping me come to know Jesus through faith. I want to thank my wife Tracie for standing by me through the past 24 years of marriage and for her love and support. I want to thank the Lord for blessing me with my two wonderful children that help me to see life more clearly. Thank you Lord that I am given the opportunity each work day, to be used as your servant to minister to those in need of hospice care.

Introduction

To me, the dying process begins the moment a patient is aware that nothing more can be done to remedy an illness and that all that stands between that moment and the time of his death, is days. The dying process can be a process of pain, while at the same time being a process of love and growth. Faith can be enriched and trust in God fortified. Family can find connection, and love for each other can spread.

Death is the one aspect of life that we can't escape. Physically we are going to close our eyes and give up our last breath. Our spirit will leave our bodies. Our families will be faced with challenges and decisions about our care needs and our dying process.

The process of dying culminates a variance of areas and problems along the way. Answers are not always available and coping and acceptance that a loved one is dying can be met with great difficulty. Having the right people in place to help guide us down the path of the dying process alleviates our fears and helps to eliminate feelings of isolation. It is this very helpful process that has drawn me to my work in the health care field and, more specifically, the calling of hospice.

I have dedicated my life to the healthcare industry for the past thirty years, with over twenty of those years in the medical field. I have degrees in mental health technology, social work, and counseling.

As a hospice social worker, I have worked with patients and their families for the past ten years and have learned a great deal from their experiences. Paying close attention to their stories has made me a better clinician. It has always been my goal to provide people with comfort and support as they endure the path before them.

Their paths are initiated in fear and apprehension and if no rally of their physical state occurs, can result in deep sadness, anticipatory grief, and a host of emotions that will not subside. Each day produces more uncertainty as the fear of death looms in the back of the minds of whom it has its grasp. As a social worker and as a fellow person who genuinely cares for people, I strive to maintain an emotional balance so that I can provide complete and focused support to my patients and their families. It is my job to help people cope with these intense feelings, guiding them within their support network and acting as an integral team member in their care.

Years of listening to family after family struggle with the question, *"What now?"* Is what has led me to write this book. My focus is to help provide insightful, basic information which I have found useful for both patients and families in the dying process. Much of the information would appear common sense. However, in the rushed world of medical care the details of dying are sometimes overtly omitted and overlooked.

I feel it is important to listen to the patient and family and follow their direction. I also have seen the benefits of educating families on how to physically and spiritually care for their loved ones at the end of life.

In the chapters ahead I will discuss my own grief reactions as a professional and the importance of self-care. I will elaborate on varied aspects of the dying process such as denial, closure, and ways to ensure a peaceful and comfortable passing.

As you read the information, allow it to settle into your thoughts as you carefully consider ways that can make you a better caregiver, provider or family member. Think about the paths that patients and families have taken over bumpy roads, busy highways and the dangerous curves that they have traveled to get to their current destination. If helpful, use analogies to process or journal your experiences. Evaluate your thoughts about death and the dying process and ways that you can reflect as you consider the value of life. I encourage you to be open to new ideas that can help to ensure that your loved one's passing is facilitated with dignity and lessened stress and tension. My audience is for those to whom death comes; the patient, his family and friends, and to those who are his caregivers. May this information be a blessing to you.

Chapter 1

Thoughts About Death

Living another day is not a guarantee for anyone. It is not as though we really have control over the day of our death, just as we had no control over the day of our birth. We are all granted a measure of time on this earth. At a young age we think about our dreams and what we will become in life. We envision graduating high school, going to college, working, getting married, having children, watching them grow up and enjoying our lives and retiring one day. We dream of our future and live our lives as though time is of no concern.

We know from the news we hear and stories of people around us that we are surrounded with danger and could at any moment succumb to an accident or by some strange unforeseen physical anomaly. I can vividly recall as a teenager losing two fellow classmates who both died in tragic accidents. The first was a full-of-life teenage girl that fell from a cliff after a thoughtless night of intoxication. The next was a young man who was hit and killed by a train. For a moment these accidents awoke me to the realization that I too am not invincible. Yet shortly thereafter I found myself closing my mind to thoughts of death and continued on with my busy life. It seems that media has reported death and dying around us so much that we have become callous and unfeeling to the grief of others.

Thinking about dying is not the most pleasant subject on which a person can dwell. In fact, it is quite disturbing. As a Christian my beliefs tell me that when I die my spirit will go on to heaven to live with Jesus. However, not all people believe the way I do, and for some who have no faith in God or an afterlife, they are left in a quandary as to if this life is all that they have.

When we lose someone, whether it be a friend, coworker, brief acquaintance, or a family member, we find ourselves pondering thoughts about death. It becomes more vivid as our emotions surface and those feelings attributed to the death of a loved one provoke thoughts and images of what our own death may be like.

Death forces us to reflect on our lives and actions. It helps to enforce acknowledgement of what is most important in our relationships and to validate our intense and overwhelming love for each other. Death causes us to negate the small stuff in life and embrace the good in our loved ones.

As a hospice social worker, I would say that there have not been many days that have gone by that I have not thought about my own death, the death of family, or the death of friends. I have thought it through many times. I don't think that it is healthy to continually dwell upon these thoughts or to live in fear, but perhaps it does help us to be conscious of our mortality and appreciate those around us of whom we love and enjoy the time we have together.

I think that my own concerns about dying are not the suffering or the pain, but moving into the unknown. I have faith in God and believe in heaven, but I have never been there so I have nothing to hold onto but my faith. I do have the peace of God, which the Bible says is a sign of His presence, and that brings me comfort.

For those that don't have faith on which to stand they may have an intense sense of loss, anxiety, and fear of death. As a Christian I am accustomed to talking about death because it is the basis of my faith. I sing hymns about leaving this world and spending eternity with Jesus. So my faith reinforces thoughts about dying, whereas other people may not practice or meditate on dying.

It's easy to see why people who have no faith would struggle with fear. Learning ways to think positively about your own death or the death of your family will help as you consider the process.

I have found that writing about working with dying people and the deaths I have experienced helps me to evaluate and put my heart into words. My job as a hospice social worker provokes me to journal and write about my experiences. I believe that it's a positive way of debriefing and processing my internal grief reactions. I like to write out poems and I wrote this one as a way of pouring out my heart so others can feel what I feel and see what I have seen.

Captured by pirates attacking my cells. Stripped naked and abused internally. My body allied with the enemy. Set a sail, in the dark of night, upon a raft of uncertainty. Isolated and cold, loneliness sets its grip into my heart. Peering upward, I fight to see, I fight to row, yet the currents and tides send me adrift in a varied flow. Heat of day and cold of night, unprotected, fatigue and weakness reduce my strength and I am shattered from within. As my body dies, my awareness of love grows. Light has the opportunity to shine and peace is obtained. My faith In God increases, as I learn to trust and let go. Accepting that death will probably surely come, I relinquish and surrender.

I find it helpful to give careful attention to the internal emotion and thoughts of those with whom I am working. Counseling draws me into that place where I can sense the pain. My approach although has to be guarded so that I maintain a healthy stance and refrain from becoming too emotionally unregulated by the hurt of those with whom I am speaking. It's my job to give strength and support and not to draw strength and energy from an already depleted patient or family member.

Who can understand or verbalize the thoughts and feelings that people experience after hearing they have a medical diagnosis of a terminal illness? Who can understand the path during the walk to death? Each of us have experienced some awareness that our life will come to a close and we will have to face the void of separation from those that we love and those who love us.

Each person is created unique, individual, independent of others, yet dependent on others. People are unique in their death, their coping, their experiences, and their life. We are born alone, yet others are present at that moment. We die alone, yet surrounded by our loved ones. We are brought into the world in love and die in love, at least this is the hope.

The process of death and dying is universal with medical and physiological changes that naturally occur within the body. Yet within the mind it brings the complication of relationships, the need for closure and peace and pain control.

The news of hearing that a loved one has a terminal, life threatening illness brings about emotions and feelings that are often very unfamiliar and unsettling. The light of day suddenly is shrouded in fear and apprehension as the future becomes very uncertain.

Attacking and tormenting thoughts invade our minds as we attempt to make sense of our life ending. We find a stirring of feelings that are often uncontrollable. These feelings manifest, appearing and exiting as they please. There is an initial awareness of disbelief and surety of overcoming this problem. We are thrust into a rush of medical consultation and decisions in the world of the unknown.

It's interesting how as people we all know that death will come to each of us at some point of our lives. We are so accustomed to living that when death comes it's often accompanied by shock and disbelief. It has been my observation that anxiety, fear, dread, apprehension and worry are some of the feelings that manifest as a result. Most people do not react in peace, joy and elation, although I have had the pleasure to be a witness to a few, who through their intense faith in God, have longed for their time to go and met it with relief and peaceful satisfaction.

Rarely have I heard the words uttered, "Oh, I'm glad that I'm dying!" or, "I'm so thankful my time has come." There are those patients who after being ill for a long time share that they are ready to go to be with the Lord or with their loved ones in heaven or that they don't want to continue to live knowing each day will be worse than the previous. This is easier to comprehend and understand because they feel a certain satisfaction with knowing their life is coming to a close.

As an unexpected tempest I have found myself breathing in the personal pain and residue of grief and anguish. Working in the hospice field with people who have mixed feelings can easily spread to my mind as I empathize with their personal pain. My heart is compassionate for those of whom I am entrusted to provide support. Hearing the stories of personal loss, physical decline and heavy hearts, I have struggled with how to cope and regenerate my energy and return day after day.

Not all of death is negative, nor are people continually full of pain. Death does bring pain, but it can also bring healthy attributes such as reconciliation, amends, family cohesion and connection while drawing family closer and reconnecting them in love. As a fire sweeping through a forest, I have seen that through the midst of death the ground of life is refurbished, seeds begin to blossom, flowers bloom and life begins again.

Chapter 2

Sudden Trauma

There are those patients and families who find themselves in a sudden unexpected event, whether it be an accident, victimization, overdose, suicide, stroke, heart attack or other. Life has been cut short and goodbyes are not often able to be spoken. These situations are emotionally taxing and full of debate and questions.

As both a medical and hospice social worker, I have worked with patients and families who have found themselves in this sudden torrent of emotion. I can recall on various occasions speaking with parents whose children were involved in accidental shootings, suicides, car accidents, overdoses, and sudden events such as strokes or heart attacks.

Finding words of comfort at such emotionally charged times leaves me praying and seeking God's help for direction and grace. Often times, just being present is all that needs to be offered.

One evening I was working the late shift at a hospital when I was called to counsel a young mom whose son was accidentally shot by his friend. I remember feeling ill equipped and just not sure how to provide help other than to be a calm, comfortable, presence. I sat across the table from her as she poured out her heart in tears. My heart broke for her as I patiently listened. Within moments the floor nurse came to her side and whisked her away to be with her son. Following our meeting I spoke with the hospital trauma chaplain to debrief. Being in these types of situations over and over, I have learned how to practice being a present, peaceful place for others to come to and rest.

Crisis situations toss patients and families to and fro, leaving them unsettled and without a sense of control or direction. Regardless of the situation or how a person starts at his place in the dying process, families can be aided through the support of one calm person. I have found that gently leading families through the process of care and preparing them for what will happen, lessens the anxiety of the unknown. In the hospice setting, families are educated about what to expect and what happens as a patient moves through the dying process.

Enduring trauma for many families occurs in baby steps. Many families will tell me that they are trusting in God and are taking life one day at a time. Thank God that in these situations we can live moment by moment. In the hospital setting life is truly in the balance and it can turn with an ever so gentle wind. It's as though bandits are in the bushes waiting to attack the frail, injured and compromised bodies of our loved ones. Infections such as C-difficile or MRSA can result in further decline to someone who is already in a weakened state.

I have seen many people come into the hospital that never leave. While an individual is in the hospital for one illness, other problems will attack and the patient will spiral down, often requiring some other form of life support. Unable to fight back, the patient's body becomes so compromised that they have to undergo life support withdraw and the patient passes in the hospital.

Meeting the needs of patients and families who are faced with sudden traumatic events can be very difficult and are met with their own host of issues. It is helpful to keep in mind by what means the patient came to his present condition when considering his needs at the time of his dying process.

Chapter 3

Talking About Death

Physicians have the difficult job of sharing with their patients that they can offer no more help. Unfortunately, some patients and families have little time to prepare for their passing. Some families have shared that in retrospect, they wish that they had not undergone treatments or taken part in treatment for the duration they had. Some patients report feeling pressured by their doctor or by other family members to continue with treatments even though they knew that they were not helping.

Sometimes patients and families hang on in hope that they will get better. However, in their waiting the miracle does not come and the person grows sicker and weaker. I remember a physician I worked with telling a patient that sometimes the miracle *is* to die and go to heaven. She noted that God answered her prayer for healing, just not in a way that she could understand. This view seems harsh to someone fighting for his life, yet over time I have seen that given all of the suffering and pain that people endure, it is often a relief when patients can just let go and surrender to death.

Yet, many people continue to seek treatment even though the doctors have explained that the treatment is palliative and not curative. It's easy to understand that people struggle with giving up. Unfortunately, in hospice care we see people who are admitted into our care the day of their death. The patient has actually been dying and either the doctor failed to tell him this or the patient and family failed to believe that he is dying.

Sometimes patients and families will sign into hospice care and then sign out the next day, saying that hospice is trying to kill them. The truth is that with or without hospice, the patient will still die. The focus of hospice is to provide comfort and quality of life as the patient transitions through the dying process.

Oftentimes individuals who have a terminal illness appear to have an acute, unexplainable awareness and understanding that their life is coming to a close and will start to make preparation. Families have shared that their loved ones started giving away personal items, asking to visit family members once more, visiting their old home place and essentially checking off their bucket list. Patients are aware that on the inside things are changing, yet for the comfort and concern of their family, they will neglect to tell them the truth. Patients appear to be aware that they are dying, yet to protect their family, they will remain silent.

In the hospital setting the majority of newly admitted hospice patients are actively dying. In this instance, there is often little time for the hospice team to quickly establish rapport, seek to control the patient's comfort and address patient and family coping and psychosocial needs.

During imminent death situations, discussions between hospice staff, patients and families often occur very quickly as they take what little time they have to participate in closure activities. Oftentimes doctors will use the palliative care team to initiate patient and family discussion about end of life care and progressing into hospice services.

Chapter 4

Pain and Loss

When we think of pain, we often consider physical pain. Yet we have most all experienced emotional pain, often stemming from loss. Within our lives we experience the pain of heartbreak, the loss of a pet, the loss of a job, the loss of a friend, the loss of a keepsake. Whatever the loss, we often feel the physical link to it within our bodies. I have found in working with people over the years that pain and loss are interconnected.

I have learned that pain is encompassed by physical, emotional, spiritual and anticipatory pain of loss. Considering all of these aspects of pain helps when the hospice team members each acts in their specialty to provide comfort and relief.

It's amazing to consider how as humans we suppress hurts and hide shameful acts. Dealing with baggage we have tried to bury or cast into the ocean, we often find it seems to find its way back to the surface. During the end of life, if these things were never dealt with, they seem to creep back and irritate us until they are resolved. Often times on an unconscious level we are affected by these problems which impact our coping and decision making ability.

The good thing about pain is that it causes us to change, to live life differently, to make amends, to forgive others, to ask God for forgiveness and to forgive ourselves.

Thoughts of losing a loved one can generate feelings and emotions that create heartache and deep feeling. I have witnessed people in grief vacillate emotionally. It is as though their mind is locked deep in the dungeon within the castle of anticipatory grief. There are levels and stairs to be climbed as they trudge between floors and move from reflection and storytelling, to a bubbling up of tears, to an explosion of feeling and releasing pent up emotion, resulting in brief calm and release. The pattern, repeating itself over and over again as pain subjugates us under its control.

Others have shared their concern of spiritual pains. These pains are associated with

27

issues about the afterlife and where a person will spend eternity. Other needs also arise, such as forgiveness or confessing hidden sin. Spiritual pains are often hidden and repressed. They cause us to act in unconventional ways and control us from within. Finding aid through the support of a chaplain is often helpful in linking the patient to their faith system. People with spiritual concerns often want to be sure that they are right with God before they die.

Emotional pains are slave masters, chaining us to their control and leading and guiding us throughout life. Our emotional losses play the movie of memories in our mind so that we dare not forget. These emotional pains remind us that we are weak and discourage us from being able to cope effectively. They have constructed dysfunctional coping mechanisms and hard wired us with maladaptive coping skills. They are often connected to feelings of guilt and self-condemnation.

Fear can be the driver of decision making and steer our loved ones already in pain and loss into added discomfort. Keep in mind that pain and loss can be linked with these hidden personality traits and affect our decisions when it comes to the dying process. Many people share that they are fearful of making decisions that will not honor promises made to the patient.

I always share with patients and families, that they are the ones who will have to live with their decisions. I add that they want to be absolutely sure and confident before making a decision they may regret. Also, I remind them that they have to live with their family and it is helpful to have as much of a group consensus as possible when making decisions regarding a patient's care needs. Families will often later communicate to me of having a release from guilt and blame as they carefully considered their choices.

Physical pain, I have found, is often an area that surprisingly few people have encountered. When I envision pain, I think of the time I suffered a gall bladder attack. I was laying on the floor at a hotel near Sea World, with my feet propped up over the corner of the bed. I was sweating and suffering with such intense cramping and sharp pains in my abdomen and back I literally thought that I was going to die. I was hurting so bad that all I could think of was relief. My wife gave me some over the counter pain medication and prayed with me as I waited it out for hours. At that moment, the only thing that helped me to feel better were my prayers to God for help, my wife at my side holding my hand and thoughts of going to heaven if I should die. I am thankful that I had the opportunity to endure this pain for the sake of empathy of others, but would not willingly choose to go through it again.

The next day I found myself sore, but because I didn't know what was happening to me, I had all sorts of questions and anxieties racing through my mind. I honestly thought it was my back. It was not until months later after having other less painful gall bladder attacks, that an ultrasound revealed that my gall bladder was full of sludge. I underwent a cholecystectomy and the problem was solved. I have spoken with women who said that their gall bladder attack hurt worse than when they gave birth to their children. This experience has helped me to be sensitive to the pain complaints of patients and to seek help when patients say they are hurting.

Pain is the one thing that can be easily remedied with medications. However, some families struggle with keeping their loved one conscious. Unfortunately their concern may be more of a selfish nature and desire to be able to communicate with their loved one. Again, thinking about the aspects of family coping and where they are in the process, I find it helpful to be patient as I offer education about pain management.

A co-worker once shared a scenario that I found helpful. She said to think about when you had the flu and imagine how you felt at the time. I imagined my stomach hurting from vomiting, body aches, feeling very weak and just wanting to stay in bed and sleep. She said now imagine that you have the flu times three and this is how our patients feel. So the question asked to me was if you feel like you have the flu, would you want to be awake and talking with visitors throughout the day? Would you want someone to try to make you eat? Would you want to try to sit up or would you just want to be left alone? Would you want the television blaring and kids running in and out of your room? Probably not. I use this as a tool to help families understand how their loved ones might be feeling.

So when thinking about your loved one's physical pain, think about how you felt when you were hurting, suffering and sick with the flu. Think about how you might feel if you were the patient, and perhaps a focus will arise to ensure that the patient is kept as comfortable as possible. I do not say this in judgment, but merely in education to help the family think about the patient and how they can aide in their comfort care.

Whenever I am with a patient and he says that his pain is a ten on a one to ten pain scale, I think of how bad I felt when I was feeling my worst pain and I am moved with compassion to help see that the patient's pain is under control.

I wonder sometimes if all people have suffered ten out of ten pain. This is the worst, most unimaginable, uncontrollable pain a person can experience. When I had my gall bladder attack, I would have considered the pain to be a ten. Having pain in our lives can be used as a very valuable tool to help us when others are suffering. As a Christian I think of the pain that Jesus suffered on the cross for mankind. The fact that He went through this to pay for my sins helps me to recognize how much He loves me. Would you suffer His kind of pain for someone you love?

It's the saddest thing to see a person writhing, moaning and suffering in pain and not be able to do anything about it. I have seen patients in the hospital setting suffer for days, directly linked to family denial, the doctor not ordering enough medication or the right types of medications coupled with a lack of knowledge about pain management by hospital nurses. I have learned that just because someone has a medical license, it does not make them an expert on pain management.

In hospice care we use different types of techniques and pain scales to evaluate pain. When patients are in the hospital under hospice care, their pain management is done by the hospital attending physician. Hospice can offer recommendations, but the care and administration of medications is based on the doctor's orders and the judgment of the nurse.

The amounts of medications that are used for pain in the hospital or nursing home setting vary from physician to physician. I have seen some cases where all that was ordered was Tylenol and other patients in a comparable condition who have a Morphine drip. Hospitals who have palliative care doctors in place seem at times to do a better job managing pain during end of life care.

There is also the way in which pain medications are ordered to be considered. Most often in the hospital setting they are ordered as needed. So it is the judgment of the floor nurse to determine if medications are needed or not. I explain to families that each nurse is different and their understanding of the dying process is different. Additionally, some nurses' struggle with administering the last dose which they feel will cause the patient's death. Whereas there are other nurses who are very on board with comfort care. These nurses know that a patient is dying and often have had prior experience to support the comfort care model and they will administer medications in a more routine manner.

The idea is to keep the patient's pain under control and unfortunately administering pain medications every five hours will not help a patient who is in extreme pain. Instead, the patient may experience peaks and valleys, where their pain will be okay for a while and then will accelerate once the pain medication has worn off. It then becomes a situation of catching up to the pain. When the next pain medication is given it takes time for the medication to take effect, leaving the patient in unnecessary discomfort. In this situation, the pain vacillates based on the medications the patient is receiving and not receiving.

Keep in mind, I am not a nurse. I have observed patients that experience these problems and I always collaborate with the hospice nurse on my team regarding medication administration and physician orders. However, over ten years I have seen patients endure pain and discomfort not because medications weren't ordered, but due to nursing conflicts about death and dying. Often there are emotional triggers for nurses who may have lost a loved one or are just not comfortable working with dying patients. The job is very emotional and it is easy to get attached to patients and their families.

Emotionally the dying process is not for every health care worker to perform. That is where hospice helps. The staff have been trained in end of life care and are comfortable in this environment.

For most people I have worked with at hospice, I find they feel their job is a calling, where God has placed them and not just a job that they wanted to do.

So when your loved one is experiencing pain, think about your own pain experiences, the medications and how and when they are administered and think about the needs of the person providing the care and the difficulties that they might be facing while caring for your loved one. Consider the benefits of hospice care and the comfort level of the people you have entrusted to keep your loved one's pain and anxiety under control.

Chapter 5

Media

The entertainment industry and media project images and circumstances that can provide false visions of the dying process. Television and movies leave out the pain and trauma associated with CPR. Death is so prevalent in media that the personal tragedy and pain associated with grieving families and friends is lost.

It is unfortunate how the local news shares of individuals who have been subjected to personal injury and death at the hand of others or by accident. I always equate that someone who loves them is grieving and in deep pain over their loss, while their information is publicly spread to an audience of people that readily toss it aside with no personal concern for the pain of the family.

People die on television and to emphasize the drama, patients receive CPR and survive. The person takes one breath and dies. People are shot and killed repeatedly in movies and television shows and there is a callous approach and loss of dignity and respect for dying people and their families.

In contrast to media representation, death that occurs in a stable setting, such as a hospital or in the patient's home, is often facilitated with hospice care. In these cases, family and loved ones have the opportunity to experience a positive passing of their family member, as they are shrouded with love. Patients are administered comfort medications and they are given a gift to die with their family around them, in a comfortable setting.

Chapter 6

Closure

I can recall after first starting in hospice care I decided to write a letter to both of my parents. In the letter I thought about my life under their care and thanked them for their love and attention. I thanked them for all of the little things that they did for me. I said that I was sorry for times when I wasn't such a nice person and I forgave them for past hurts. I mentioned little details of my mom taking me downtown and for rides on the bus. I thanked her for giving me change to buy a soft drink or candy. I tried to recall significant events in my life to help her remember also.

As I typed my thoughts, feelings started to emerge and my heart began to flow with more concrete ideas. I found it as a positive way of making preparation for the future and at the same time giving me the chance for closure. I could not say whether or not I would be able to be with my parents at the time of their death. I was able to say what I needed to say in writing.

I wrote a letter both to my mom and to my dad. My parents live roughly nine hundred miles away and I started to consider that they were growing old and that I may not see them when they die, so I didn't want to have anything left unsaid. I mailed my letter to my dad and when I came home to visit my mom, I read the letter to her. It was a beautiful moment, for it brought her to tears.

I mailed my letter to my dad, who at the time was undergoing heart surgery. I didn't want to run the chance that he would die and I would have held in my feelings for him. The letter I wrote to my mom I completed later. I wanted to read it to her when I went for a visit.

Looking back in time, I am so thankful that I took that step. My mom now has dementia and does not even recognize who I am. Had I not said what I needed to say at that time, it would be too late. It was my hope that in expressing my thoughts about her, that I could help her to

41

understand my appreciation of her giving birth to me, washing clothes, and being there for me behind the scenes. I wanted her to understand my thankfulness for her sacrifices and giving heart. Again, I am so thankful that I shared my feelings with her. It's something I'll never regret.

Sometimes in life families wait until the last moment to say what they really need to say to their loved ones. Hurts and times of bitter feelings result in separation. I have spoken with people who for whatever reason, live estranged from each other for years and at the last moment will make amends. There are of course others who have no regard for closure and do not respond when their family member or friend is dying. During life bridges are burned and sometimes the pain is too great to reconcile those past hurts.

I recall hearing a story from a preacher who said that after years of physical abuse from her father, God told her to forgive him, but also to thank him for giving her life. She noted that this journey took time and patience, yet she found a release within her when she expressed her heart.

For me, a healing took place inside as I cleared the slate of past situations that I may have been involved in that could have caused hurt feelings.

Regardless of the stage of life that we are in, it is never too early or too late to take advantage of the time that we have and tell our loved ones how we feel about them. Writing a letter for me was the one way that I could give my parents something that they could keep and reflect on.

Taking action in the steps of closure is a process. I want to talk about the important aspects of dying and preparing oneself for the loss of a loved one. In hospice care I find myself every day in a hospital room with family gathered around the patient's bed. The patient is often too weak to participate in closure activities. However in some instances a patient can respond and interact with their family. In my years of working with hospice patients I have instituted the following aspects of closure as a part of my practice.

The following stages are very important and helpful to both patients and family. They are not to be utilized in any certain order or to use at any certain time. They are simply considerations to implement, to help in the closure process. Please read through these stages and take part as you choose. These are aspects of closure that I have learned and encourage families to initiate as they go through the dying process.

Being Able to Say Goodbye

It is important to create space to speak your heart and bring up those deep feelings from within that you might otherwise be afraid to speak. I encourage you to share them with a genuine heart and full emotion. Children can benefit from sitting or lying beside their loved one, touching them and speaking with their loved one. I have seen many a family member get in bed with the patient. It is such an intimate time and should be permitted when applicable.

There are of course those times when due to patient contact isolation needs or risk of exposure to transferring some form of infection or disease that it is not warranted. However, families who spend that time alone with their loved ones can speak their hearts to each other and be at peace.

There may be adults who may have been estranged or not spoken in years. It is important to speak one's heart not in anger, but in gentleness and with compassion. It is an understanding that not all family members have had the best of relationships with their loved ones and that there may be feelings of guilt, hurt, pain or abuse. It is a matter of individual direction about disclosure and what needs to be said or not said. Often times there could be a child who is in prison or a family member overseas. Attempting to make contact and allowing family time to say goodbye can be very helpful for both the family and the patient.

Many family members, due to location and inability to travel, can use the phone to speak their love to the patient and say their goodbyes. I have worked with multiple family members who were in jail or in prison who did not have the opportunity to leave. So setting up a phone call with the facility chaplain at the prison provided aid to the inmate and also allowed them the support of the chaplain following the call.

Being able to say goodbye provides the opportunity to express thanks to the patient for their love and help to validate their role in the life of the family member. It is a positive way to let go and move forward.

Permission to Go

It is important to share statements like, *"It's okay"* or *"I'll be alright"*. It is okay to say, *"I'll miss you"* or *"Let go when you are ready"*. This allows a peace within the patient and resolves conflicts between the patient being ready to die and fighting to remain because the family doesn't want to let them go.

I have seen families struggle with saying it is okay to go and I have seen dying patient's holding on until their family member released them. One day I was working on a case where a patient's husband stood over her bed and said, *"Don't leave me"* over and over again. The patient was unconscious, but very restless. My co-worker and I said a prayer and soon afterwards the husband's pastor walked into the room. His pastor spoke with him about letting go and within what seemed like just a few moments, the spouse changed his mind and told his wife that it was okay for her to go. Immediately she calmed down, relaxed, became very peaceful and slipped away. I wouldn't have believed it if I had not seen it with my own eyes, but over my career in hospice care, I have seen this happen repeatedly.

This holding on by families creates anxiety and often can manifest in terminal restlessness where the patient appears anxious or unsettled. Patients can read their families and will hold on even though they are ready to die. It is important for the family to convey in honesty that it is okay for the patient to go and also ensure the patient that they will be okay. It is a true gift of unselfishness to express permission to go.

Resolving Hurts and Expressing Your Love

Consider the value of making amends and saying I'm sorry. Offer up your heart and submit yourself to say I forgive you and please forgive me. Express your love by saying *"I love you"* and *"thank you!"* Expressions of affection and devotion can help that connection at end of life. It is helpful to express feelings both in person and over the telephone. Even if the patient is unresponsive, it is helpful to speak to the patient and disclose these things. Families may feel like the patient cannot hear them or it is too late.

While the patient is still living, having the opportunity to say what is needed creates a space of healing and expression of the heart. Some families may find it helpful to speak to the patient, whereas others may write their feelings down in a letter. Whatever you choose to do, having said what is needed will help so that the family member has no regrets of what they wished they would have said to their loved one.

Individual Time Alone With the Patient
For Adults and Children

A very important step is taking time to be with the patient and allow space with the patient, either in the bed, beside the bed or holding hands.

Taking time alone allows the person and patient to speak their love and their hearts with intimacy. These messages of love and honesty again bring peace and closure. When I am working with families I always ask if each member has had time alone with the patient and without an audience so they can fully disclose their love, without the judgment or opinion of others.

We all have a need for privacy and there are things that only the patient needs to hear from individual family members. It is unfortunate in some cases where one person will dominate the space around the bed and decide who speaks to the patient and who doesn't. I have seen cases where the patient's second wife will not disclose to other family members the extent of a patient's illness, cutting them out of the opportunity for closure. It is sad to think that someone would have to maintain such a high level of control.

During another case that I worked on, the patient's wife did not get along with the patient's children and was seriously considering not calling the patient's son and daughter to tell them that he was dying. When I learned this I strongly suggested she concede and via telephone I called the son who was out of state, allowing him time to talk to his dad through phone closure. I also assisted in supporting family by calling his daughter who was local, allowing her time to see her dad. Interestingly enough, the patient had been taken off of life support and was nonresponsive. This individual appeared to be holding on. After having contact with his two children, the patient died just moments later. Allowing that brief time of intimacy can strongly affect the death of patient. I have observed this same scenario hundreds of times as patients prepare for their passing.

Religious Faith Systems

Be aware that ensuring that a patient's spiritual needs are met to assure peace and closure, preparedness and forgiveness and right standing with God are often very sacred and holy to the patient. Many times I have worked with co-workers who not having a particular religion or belief system, overlook the importance of closure from a faith perspective.

I am very sensitive to this area and ensure that the patient and family has the support that they need, whether it be through a hospice or hospital chaplain, through a pastor, priest or someone through their own faith system.

Many times people carry with them regard for past sins, actions, and deeds committed that they feel intense blame, guilt and self-condemnation. Allowing contact from a spiritual leader, can help bring forgiveness and a preparation to leave this world.

I have been present many times as the Catholic priest administers prayers, preparing the release of the patient's spirit back to God. It is a beautiful time for the patient and family and supports spiritual closure.

Family Presence

It is important to create an environment for the patient that reflects the personality and individuality of the patient. Some families are jovial and some are serious. Some speak openly in front of the patient and others are quiet and respectful. Continue to act in a manner that the patient enjoyed. Keep in mind that the patient may benefit from a presence that it is more calm and serene, with low light, soft music, and few visitors. Whereas some patient's would want the window shades up, the sun shining and the television on. Be sensitive to the patient's needs. Some patients will wait until their family arrives to pass.

I have noticed how patients who are sedated and uncommunicative will calm down when they hear the voice of their loved ones. Family will stand by their side and rub their hand and head, offering comforting words. In some cases, family will tell funny stories about the patient and the patient will calm down. Their breathing will slow down and they will become more relaxed.

In some situations I have seen the opposite occur, where a calm patient will suddenly become alarmed and fearful when their family enters the room. In this situation, it presents concerns that the family may have not had a good relationship with the patient and the patient may be fearful of their presence. Sometimes the patient may not want family in the room and their anxiety will heighten. It is interesting how at times patients who are sedated and unresponsive to staff will appear to sense their families' presence and their anxiousness and restlessness abates.

I have also experienced how patients will hold on until their family arrives from out of town, as though they are waiting for them to get to the hospital before passing. Some might feel that this is a coincidence, however, as many times as I have witnessed this same situation, I feel that there is truth to it.

I would have you strongly encourage family members to visit or call and complete closure over the telephone or video chat if possible. I have seen this happen with patients who are completely nonresponsive. The family member will make the call as another family member holds up the phone to the patient's ear and within minutes a patient who has been holding on for days, will pass.

So carefully consider the patient's needs regardless if they are able to communicate. Be aware that the patient's hearing is the last sense to go and allow both the conscious and unconscious patient the honor and opportunity for closure.

Family Absence

During the dying process sometimes patients will wait until their family leaves the room to pass. I have observed that families will sit with a patient day after day and hour after hour and the moment they step out for a bite to eat or a cup of coffee, their loved one will pass. It is as though the patient is protecting the family from the experience of witnessing their death and waits for a time when they are alone to leave.

I once went on a death visit where the patient had died and his family told me that the patient was completely alert and expressed to his daughter his thanks to her for caring for him and said that it would be her job to take care of her mom. She said that he had told her that he would be leaving very soon. She said that she stepped out into another room of her home and when she returned to her dad's room, he had died. Sometimes patient's will prepare their family members for their passing. In this instance, the daughter did not think that his death would have occurred so rapidly, but as the patient told her he was leaving he waited until she was out of the room and he died. I have experienced this same situation with other patients throughout my career and used this scenario as a standard example.

So if your loved one is holding on and family have camped out in their room, consider stepping away for a moment and see if any change occurs. I am always amazed at how this simple consideration will often result in a patient's passing.

Getting Personal Affairs in Order

Various concerns arise as patients prepare for their passing and family may need assistance with tying up loose ends, getting affairs in order and completing business matters.

The patient who is conscious may inquire about financial needs and completing a revised will or being assured that their loved one's financial needs are met. Often times the patient was the person who took care of the household finances and there needs to be a passing of the torch, so to speak.

Patients may be concerned about their funeral plans and may want to write or need help writing their obituary. They may ask to wear certain clothes or want a certain song or poem read at their funeral. Some people attempt to lessen the burden on their families by having everything in place when they die.

Many people find that the less burden they can place on their family, the better they feel about leaving. It is a great concern for many patients to have their affairs in order, whereas some people are not as concerned.

Families have shared that their mom or dad never openly talked about dying, so they never made funeral plans, a will, or advance directives leaving the family responsible to make decisions.

This focus seems to add more tension and stress to an already stressful situation. Feelings of anger can surface as the tolls of after-death care arise, whereby a family is left with the business matters of the patient.

While conducting bereavement calls following the death of patients I have heard countless people share about the financial concerns that are involved following the death of their loved one. Many times the family reports being left holding the burdens of the patient's financial responsibilities which adds to their grief.

I have found it useful to tell families to start to plan early and speak about the patient's wishes, prior to their passing. Completing advance directives and answering questions about what to do if a loved one dies or should become ill, will help alleviate the guilt and stress added to an already difficult situation.

Consider utilizing the time that you have now to make plans for the future and put directives in place about what you want done, how it should be done, and who can be trusted to carry out those wishes. There are all types of advance directives a patient can utilize and are available either online or through area hospitals, hospices, or even doctor offices. Just keep in mind that the more information the patient can verbalize or scribe to their family early on will aide as they prepare for their passing later.

To me, my own parents are role models for what aging parents should do prior to their need for care and in preparation for their death. I can remember them always talking openly about their death and what the kids should do if they are ever in a particular situation. Thankfully they have taken steps to assign one of my siblings as durable power of attorney and have completed their funeral plans.

In instances where patients have their affairs in order, it creates a very smooth transition where everything has been laid out on the table and the puzzle is complete. It is hard for families, when their loved ones never spoke about dying or what they wanted done regarding funeral plans or advance directives, to carry out end of life care.

Many patients who have not provided information to their family about end of life decisions will create a great deal of stress and emotional strain for their loved ones if they force them into having to make decisions on their behalf. It is very helpful when patients have either spoken about their end of life wishes or have completed a living will.

A living will is a written advance directive that clearly states a patient's wishes should they require life support. The patient can clearly indicate to family what they would or would not want done if in a specific medical situation. Living will information is available online and forms can easily be printed off for patient and family use. Again, consider openly conversing with your loved ones about their wishes so that when end of life conditions present themselves, you will have some clear direction about what to do.

Chapter 7

Barriers to Acceptance

Patients struggle with acceptance of their illness, acceptance of their mortality, and acceptance of making advance directives in preparation for their death. Families too are caught in the whirlwind of roadblocks which affect their decision making abilities. I have included some common barriers that occur as patients' transition in their illness and move into the dying process.

Feelings of Guilt

This is probably one of the most common issues that originates when speaking with families. Guilt and self-condemning thoughts about promises made to the patient arise. *I promised I would never put them in a nursing home. I promised I would always let them live in their house. I promised them I would never let them die in the hospital.* These promises are often made at a time in life when both the patient and their family were at a different place emotionally, mentally, and physically.

These thoughts plague families and dealing with these feelings create barriers to moving forward. Many people deal with feeling guilty about varied areas of care. The focus from a hospice perspective is to help the family through normalization and education.

Often times talking through the feelings of guilt and helping people to see the reality of their guilt will lance the problem and create release from the pressure of this infection-like stronghold.

For example, I can recall a situation where a family member made a promise to the patient that he would never put her in a nursing home. At the time of the promise the patient and her family member were younger and at a different place in life. The patient now in her nineties, and her child now in his seventies, can no longer honor the promise. The child in his seventies has health issues of his own and cannot care for the patient due to his own physical limitations, nor do they have the financial resources any longer to pay for

61

24/7 private caregivers. The family support system they once had is now dissolved and the child still is carrying this promise around like an anchor of guilt.

The patient requires nursing home placement following the fracture of her hip with increased dementia and will need prolonged custodial care in the long term care setting. Processing the reality of the situation and helping families by normalizing the concern can aid in helping the family move forward with nursing home care. Families may or may not be able to extinguish their guilt, but through education and helping their child to process the truth about the patient's care needs helps to alleviate these feelings of guilt.

I have come to recognize that people come into my care with a lifetime of problems and it is not my job to fix their every problem, but to instead help them move forward, ensuring that their loved one has their needs met in the best possible setting available.

When it comes to the dying patient, I pray and ask for God's guidance to help the patient and his family with finding resolution and healing of guilt. We never know why people feel the ways they do and it is not my position to have to come to their rescue. As a hospice social worker I have to tackle the problem at hand and let the others fall by the way side. Time, unfortunately, is slipping away and the needs of the patient are often the primary focus.

Feeling Responsible for The Patient's Death

A major concern spoken by families is feeling responsible for their loved one's death. In consideration of this concern, it has been my experience that the person will expire either with or without life support. Life support is the means by which a person is provided medications, respiratory, nutritional, dialysis or other implemented actions to artificially support normal bodily functions which require help to continue to support life.

It's helpful to give voice to families who won't say, *"I feel like I am killing my loved one"*. Normalizing this grief response is helpful to families so that they do not feel alone or unique in their situation. It appears to provide families with a lessening of worry when they know that there are other people who feel the same way. Again, many people carry with them strong convictions. For those with faith in God I always ask to pray with them that God will give them a peace or a knowing of absolute surety of their decisions before they have to make them. I encourage them to speak to their loved one's doctors and to gain as much information as possible before making such an intense life changing decision. The majority of times, within a day or so, family will respond and decide with confidence either one way or the other.

Many people coming into hospice care, will say that they feel like they are giving up if they stop treatments. This feeling comes out even though the doctor has told them that nothing more can be done.

Helping people of faith go to the root of their concerns and seek God's direction helps them to feel at peace with their decision making. Now not all people have faith in God, so prayer may not be helpful. For families who don't hold to a faith system, often times it helps to have clear information to evaluate the patient's condition and this can be done by speaking as a family with the patient's medical team.

Working with both types of patients and families, I stress setting up a family conference with the doctor and medical team and ask straight forward questions about the patient's condition and prognosis, treatment options, and the doctor's recommendations. Sometimes families don't hear the first or second time what the doctor has told them, so it is helpful to have multiple family members present to hear what the doctor has to say.

When families can participate together in medical conference, the information presented can help lessen the feeling of responsibility, knowing that death is not in their hands to decide or that death is imminent, regardless of their decision.

I think back on a patient that I had many years ago in the nursing home who had developed a life-changing illness at an early age. His spouse struggled with comfort care and was conflicted about decisions regarding withdrawing his feeding tube or reinserting it when the patient pulled it out. His care needs continued to increase and his condition continued to decline. After months and months of education about comfort care, his spouse shared that God had given her the answer that she needed and she was able to move on in peace over her decision to withdraw her spouse from life support.

I always share with families that when the time to allow death comes, that they will have a knowing that it is time. Helping remove the guilt of feeling responsible for a loved one's death can be supported with education about the reality of the patient's condition and helping family recognize that the death of their loved one will occur regardless of their decision. Helping to normalize this grief response may aide the family as they travel around this barrier.

Personal Concerns

Concern for one's own wellbeing and emotional health are sometimes driving mechanisms when it comes to being able to let our loved one go. I have witnessed that a family's worry about financial concerns, such as how they would be able to continue to live without the support of their spouse, dependents being left needing a caregiver, or even adult children who have lived with the patient and who are unemployed or disabled may suddenly discover that they will be homeless if they decide to stop care.

Placing no judgment on anyone, I have seen cases where when patients die, it leaves family members in great psychosocial distress. There are primary financial needs that create problems with meeting monthly bills, assisting with nutrition and need for food, clothing and the basics of life.

Ethical situations arise where it is questionable if the family is acting in the best interest of the patient or if they are possibly keeping the patient at home and doing everything for them to keep them alive so that they can keep a roof over their own head. Again it is not my place to judge. My focus is to help the patient and family with their needs. I would not want to be in their shoes.

Looking back many years as a new social worker I was more into rules, but now after seeing people at their worst, I keep a healthy space away and try to look at life from the whole picture. I give more grace, and ask how I can be of assistance. It's a proper thing to respect people's wishes and not dwell on my own thoughts of what I would do. Sometimes in the hospital and hospice world a lot of opinion is dispersed. I try to always keep in mind that it's not about me, but it's all about this family. I am just here to help them anyway I can.

Be conscious of the fact that not everyone thinks and acts as you do. Give consideration and grace to patients and families and treat them with dignity. Help them through education and respect their position on end of life care, whatever form it may take.

Be alerted that concern-for-self will occur within families as the thought of their support system being removed affects their well-being. Seek ways to assist family members and evaluate other support systems that can assist them after the death of their loved one. Occasionally this can be provided by the hospital or hospice social worker through resource allocation.

Code Status

There are those families who regardless of the type of education and instruction provided, will agree to sign an advance directive to allow their loved one to die without first undergoing a full code. It is unfortunate that families feel this way, and it is most often observed that patients and families who refuse to sign a *Do Not Resuscitate* or *Allow Natural Death* order, often die a traumatic death either at home, on the way to the hospital, or in the hospital. At times patients and families are torn with barriers that are affecting their decisions such as: fear of death, guilt, feeling responsible and denial.

Having been personally educated about the actual survival statistics of patients who endure respiratory and cardiac arrest codes might help patients and families think otherwise. In my work at hospice I keep an information sheet about the extremely minimal survival rates for patients with terminal illnesses. Terminally ill patients who undergo CPR or intubation rarely survive.

Many times the doctor, hospital, and hospice teams have provided thorough education to the family about code status, and yet the family still decides to keep their loved one a full code. At this point it is helpful to evaluate the goals of the family and whether hospice is what they really want or not. Some people use hospice care for the services they provide and not because they are ready to die.

There are often hidden barriers that families have and that regardless of how much instruction is provided, they will not concede to completing code status forms. I have found that in time families will come to that place of acceptance and proceed with a no code status.

The thought of signing a no code status for some families means that they are giving up or they have just written a death sentence. I think many people have a subconscious fear that if they sign a DNRO the patient will die, or if they make funeral plans, the patient will die. I have had some families tell me this very thing.

Some families are concerned about how they will cope with the absence of their loved one. The emotional pain associated with the thought of losing their loved one pushes them into a position of denying what is happening. This denial occurs so they can alleviate their own pain and discomfort over the situation. Due to this denial, they avoid all conversations related to signing a no code status.

I have also seen families avoid coming to the hospital at specific times of the day when doctors or medical staff may ask them about code status. Additionally, I have observed families that refuse to answer the phone when they see phone numbers from the hospital. These families are practicing avoidance in hopes that the ending they are dreading will somehow fade away.

Be aware that signing a code status does not initiate death, it is just a tool, set in place to prevent a patient from suffering a painful, traumatic death, when it comes.

Patients and families who have mentioned that they want everything done typically will sign out of hospice care. In the cases that it is the patient's desire to be a full code, there are obviously issues that the patient is not discussing. In many of these cases the patient may say something like, *"If I'm going to die, I want to try everything possible to stay alive."*

Consider the thought processes of patients and families and recognize that some patients and families struggle with electing a no code status. Education can be provided, but often times there are unseen issues that families struggle with that hinder their moving forward in the dying process.

Chapter 8

How We Cope

Utilizing effective ways to cope with our loved one's illness will help us during the dying process. Personally, I have used writing as a means of self-expression. Journaling has helped me to process the deep emotions that correspond with the losses that a family may experience. I have found it helpful to use analogies to put into stories or poems how I think that others may feel about their illness or the dying process. Words and their meaning help me to express my grief reactions from a positive place. I have added the following that I wrote as an example.

In a moment of calm and of silence, I sit at your bedside and listen to the cadence of your breathing. For a moment my mind has found rest. I awaken to the alarm of your ventilator. A surge of adrenaline, my tense body is startled and I am awoken and reminded of reality. Two months of sitting and watching,

74

hoping and praying, seeking and staying. Thoughts of the doctor sharing that nothing more can be done revolve in my mind and I feel a great sense of fear. My heart aches from thoughts of you leaving. We have been together all of our life. Memories flood my vision and dread and anxiety cling to my body. Hours until the time where you will sail away from me, from all sight you will pass and these last moments will be all that I can recall. Life in a land of white deserts, where wild plants are covered in thorns and small life sustaining flowers. The harshness of medical war has left the forest around me callous, unfeeling, traumatized and cold from the fierce tempest storms. Bright shades of royal flood the night's skies and energy and encouragement pierce my wearied eyes. Numbness and confusion, tears and emptiness are met with breath taken from your lungs. I peer over your body and block the sounds of a cold medicinal room, where many have journeyed before. You have surrendered your fight and left me alone. I am led from the place where you are, forever separated from the sound of your heart. I long for your warm hug, for the love of your life. Had I only known I would have given you your time. Time to be at home. Time to spend alone. A time to see the Sun. A time for life and fun. The time of our youth where we were free to live, now stripped away, as my heart's pain never seems to fade. Yet I express gracious prayers for the ones who came to aide, to take away your anxiety and to take away your pain. Forever I am thankful and I will never forget, the day you said goodbye as angels held us both in their soft and gentle wings.

Others may find that painting, gardening, walking, talking, or participating in a hobby offers a release from the stresses of caregiving. Regardless of what you do to help create an outlet during the dying process, keep in mind positive ways to express yourself and maintain balance in your life.

During a patient's illness the ways in which both the patient and family cope often differ. Finding effective ways to cope with the daily stresses of illness and care can at times be difficult. I have found that many patients and families report using medications such as anti-depressants or anti-anxiety medications. Patients of course are often limited in their activities of daily living and therefore lose their ability to drive and get around as they once did. Many patients are confined to their home, so their activity is even minimized the more. Activity may be sitting on the front porch, watching television, reading, listening to the radio or visiting with family and friends.

Due to the needs of the patient, caregivers may be restricted to their home with little social contact or ability to find respite from the role of caregiving. Finding a healthy outlet whereby stress and tension can be released is often a challenge.

Caretakers often express feeling the strains of anxiety and worry as a part of their 24/7 care. They lose precious sleep and emotions are heightened as the patient's needs become greater, so accessing an outlet for personal time can help to achieve some balance and rehydration to a dried up reserve.

I have found that working in hospice care can at times be emotionally draining. It is not as though I am really doing anything special or physically challenging, yet being in an atmosphere whereby patients and family are experiencing intense grief and anxiety seems at times to catch hold of my emotional strength and zap my energy. I have to maintain a healthy balance of rest and times away from caregiving to be able continue providing ongoing support.

I find myself amazed how people stand up under the pressures of caring for their loved ones. Love and good intentions will only take a caregiver so far. There has to be a balance and rest from the tolls that overextend our minds and body. Utilizing effective coping mechanisms will help the caregiver and patient.

Some families appear to benefit from sleep, respite care, psychosocial counseling and emotional support. Others may use the support of their pastor, church or faith system and through the use of prayer. Many individuals find a reprieve in exercise, personal hobbies, or through education by learning more about their loved one's illness.

I have entered many patients' rooms and found a family member burned out, stressed out, and wiped out from seemingly never ending care. I try to sit with these families and just let them ventilate. Their emotions may be a juggled mess, yet sometimes just being able to carry on a conversation whereby someone can pour out their heart brings a release in the soul. During these sessions people will express having a peace come over them and say that they feel better.

Of course there is always the healthy cry. I thank God for the ability to cry. I see it as the pressure valve of our body. It helps to release pent up feelings and emotions that if held in would surely suffocate us and add to our grief.

Unfortunately, there are negative outlets such as drinking alcohol in excess, chronic worry, fear and panic attacks. Some people respond to their grief in anger. Often times I find myself at the other end of a loaded gun of emotion where families fire back in what we call displaced anger. The person is angry about his loved one dying and he takes it out on whoever enters into his path.

It is vital that patients and families find healthy alternatives to cope with their stress through means that will provide a positive release of energy and incorporate a recharge to continue on in care.

Chapter 9

The Dying Process

This is another poem that I wrote to help me think about the dying process.

My body, too weak to draw a breath, my heart strained and decreasing in strength. Thoughts circle within my spirit. My mind is numb and energy is depleted. My extremities lay still and my life lays silently. Internal conversations and intimate prayers. Speaking to God. Voices pass by me and my focus diminished. Paralyzed I shout and I cry, yet no one can hear me as I strive to survive. Separation is initiated and I am free of my pain, moving into the light of God's presence and love.

I have been with thousands of patients in the dying process and been an observer of their actions, words, thoughts and beliefs. There are those few instances where God has revealed the mysteries of death. However, the majority are hidden in a shroud of privacy and secrecy. I have had those small, short glimpses, where I have been able, without question, to see God's hand at work. Yet in the midst of a culmination of deaths, I have seen that God extends His grace to families who get time with their loved ones before they die. In the flurry of emotion and activity it is easy to fail to recognize the gift that has been given to us.

During the dying process in the final moments of life, we see physical changes occurring such as respirations increasing or decreasing, secretions in the throat and lungs, mottling of fingers and toes, decreased urine output, dehydration, no desire to eat or drink, restlessness, and anxiety and pain. These issues are often easily remedied with comfort medications. During the dying process medications are given for pain, anxiety, and breathing and to assist in drying up secretions and mouth care is provided. Emotional care and family support are the focus.

In hospice care we use various scales to determine if a patient is uncomfortable. One particular scale monitors the comfort for a patient who cannot respond or is nonresponsive. As a hospice social worker it is my job to ensure that patients are not exhibiting signs or symptoms of discomfort and report back to the hospice nurse who is also working with the patient. My other role is to provide emotional support and active listening to families and friends and to support closure activity.

As a family member your only job should be to love the patient. I always respect the time that families have with their loved ones and keep my interviews short and to the point. Sometimes family require that I hold their hand, pray with them, or stay with them for extended periods of time for support.

When I visit with a family I give them the time that they require and open myself up to be a servant to their needs. However I can help, I offer to do so. As a family member or friend, you can do the same for your loved ones. Just being a presence in the room is sometimes all that is needed.

While spending time with families who are going through the dying process there may be periods of silence. This is okay. You don't have to feel the need to continuously talk, saying something or asking questions. I try to keep the conversation on the patient and family and rarely will I add something about myself, unless the family requests information. When family asks me a question, I see this as a moment for the family to take a break from the heaviness of their grief and to spiral off for a moment into a less interrogating subject.

Again, just practice being present and offer help as needed. Respect family time with the patient and limit your visit to the need at hand. Try not to overstay your welcome.

Be aware of the patient's physical needs. Most hospices will provide information to families about what is happening as their loved one goes through the dying process and this information can help family eliminate false perceptions of what will happen. Many families have shared that the information provided about end of life care really helped them to understand what was going on.

Chapter 10

Children

One of the saddest situations that I find myself to be involved with is the death of a parent and helping her children. This is probably because I am a parent and can empathize with the difficulties these families are facing. Throughout my time at hospice I have been involved with terminal ventilator weans and parents dying from cancer and all forms of illness. I have been with families immediately following the death of their loved one in the home setting as well as in the nursing home and hospital settings. Adults bring challenges of their own, but helping children face the loss of their loved one can be even more challenging.

Many parents will ask if they should allow their child to speak to or see a dying patient; and from a hospice perspective, closure is always recommended. It is of course the prerogative of the family and their judgment based on their knowledge of their children and how they feel that they will react. Many parents elect to not allow a visit from their younger children due to the image of seeing their mom or dad in a diseased state. Other families remain present with their children when visiting their loved one. The most important thing is to use your own judgment based on your knowledge of your child's emotional health and maturity.

When it comes to coping, it is normal to cry. When I am with a family member and they start to cry, I do not rescue them from crying freely, by offering tissues. Sometimes a good heart cry needs to be uninterrupted. It is not my job to stop a person from feeling the pain and grief that they are feeling, but to encourage the expression of their innermost feelings. I was taught in my counseling program that offering a tissue creates a break in the emotion and moment and that it is better to have tissues nearby before initiating a conversation with a family member.

Be aware of changes in your child's behavior such as insomnia, mood changes, withdraw, avoidance, flat affect or stoicism, chronic crying or a lack of interest. Utilize the support of those who are providing your family member with care. Social workers and child life specialists are often offered as support workers and can aide with the administration of pre and post bereavement literature and resource information. Be sure to access the support of your child's guidance counselor for in-school support.

Young children can be aided in their coping by making memories of their loved one through creative activities such as drawing a picture, tracing out their loved one's hand and then tracing their hand in their mom or dad's hand. Other ideas include drawing pictures or writing a story. Some families will do shadow boxes or scrapbooks. My family actually did some video and voice recordings of the patient telling stories. Some people may find it helpful to do photography. I had one person show me a photograph of him and his grandfather hugging just before he died.

These ideas are found on the internet and whatever you choose to do, there is no right or wrong method, but aiding children in making memories will help them with the dying process.

As I said earlier, be aware that some hospitals and hospices may offer child life specialists who are trained professionals who can help with children's grief and coping issues. Social workers are also valuable assets in working with children and their coping needs. Following the death of the patient hospices offer bereavement care and camps for children who have lost a family member. Bereavement counselors can help children and parents with coping following the death of a loved one.

On occasion children can be overlooked and supporting them by asking their caregivers questions about closure activities helps the parents to leave their grief and think about the needs of their grieving children.

Many times I will be involved with a case where a patient will be undergoing a wean from a ventilator and children will be at the bedside. In some hospitals children are not allowed to be present at the time of or following death. Keep in mind the needs of children as they too are grieving and are in need of support.

It is important to keep in mind that children are not just kids between the ages of 1 and 18, but also adult children, children with special needs, dependent children, and surrogate children. I have come to learn that the age of a parent's death does not lessen the pain of facing loss. Sometimes the pain may be greater due to the expanse of time a relationship has developed.

I have worked with some adult children who have lived with their parent all of their life and are at a complete loss when their mom or dad dies. They may have been their caregiver and were dependent on their parent for their housing or sustenance. I try to keep in mind that regardless of the age of a child, they are still the child of their loved one who is dying and leaving them.

Chapter 11

Estranged Family

Within families there are fractured relationships, which often result in separation and estrangement. Family members do not speak for months or years and at the time of death their relationships are not always mended.

Often time's families feel embarrassed or provide lack of consideration or concern for family members who are estranged such as those in jail, prison, or homeless. It has been my experience that asking the hospice social worker to contact the prison, a chaplain can support a positive outcome for phone closure.

I have been involved in several cases related to family members in prison and have always been met by cooperation with prison chaplain support.

Other times families have been torn apart from issues such as divorce, substance abuse, alcoholism, mental illness, and past hurts.

Whatever the cause, there are those patients who hope to make amends with their loved ones. Some situations have been damaged far too long to recover and patients and families will express a *why bother* attitude.

It seems at times that within each family there is always one person who is the black sheep and one from whom family never hears. Providing an estranged family member the opportunity for notification provides that person the option for closure and reconciliation. In many cases the estranged person can be reached and with technologies and search engines and social media sites, people are a little easier to be located.

Some patients with whom I have worked with have shared that they hoped to make amends with their loved ones, but at this stage of their life, they are tired of waiting and are indifferent as to the importance of participating in closure. The same holds true to family who have remained estranged by choice and feel that because their loved one never cared about them throughout their life, why bother now.

There are those times where supporting closure should be offered as an opportunity to both patient and the estranged family member(s). I have seen the few cases where a child will reconcile with his loved one and live on in peace. It is always helpful to see if assistance can be offered in helping family make contact with estranged family to identify closure needs.

Chapter 12

Good Death – Bad Death

In hospice care we consider scenarios of patients that experience a good death and those whom experience a bad death. The differences between the two are the way in which the patient and family elect the ways they die. They involve barriers to acceptance regarding the diagnosis and prognosis and psychosocial issues that influence decision making. They include aspects of age and family, coping, and readiness of patient and family.

In the following two scenarios, I present two extremes, one being negative, whereby patient and family are struggling with the dying process and scenario two, where the patient and family have made preparation and are ready to accept death. Neither of these two scenarios are from actual case studies. Both are fictional examples.

Scenario # 1

Medical Assessment

Mr. Smith is a 55 year old, white, married, male, who is Christian by faith. Mr. Smith was diagnosed with stage 3 lung cancer 9 months ago. He has undergone both chemotherapy and radiation treatments. He was currently admitted to the hospital with respiratory distress and initially required bi-pap support and later transitioned to full ventilator support. Three attempts have occurred to wean Mr. Smith from the ventilator with no success. Mr. Smith is alert and oriented to person place and time. The medical team has spoken with Mr. Smith regarding his current prognosis and had found that he wants to be weaned from the ventilator and be allowed to die a comfortable death under hospice care. A referral has been made to hospice care for evaluation.

Social Work Assessment

Mr. Smith is married and has 3 children, ages 20, 16 and 8. He is the oldest of 6 siblings. He was self-employed. His wife does not work and has been the patient's sole caregiver for the past 9 months. They have nearly exhausted their savings and have been receiving financial assistance from family. This hospice social worker met with the patient and his wife and other family today for a hospice information visit. I provided the patient and family with information about the hospice philosophy of care. The patient has verbalized by nodding yes or no, to his physicians that he wants to undergo a compassionate wean.

During our meeting the patient's wife verbalized that she is not in support of the patient coming off of the ventilator and feels that with prayer and time, the patient will improve. She encourages the patient to follow her plan and he concedes. Two of the patient's brothers are in full support of the patient's wishes, whereas three sisters are not. There is a great deal of tension and dissention among the family. I was advised that the patient's wife lost her mom and dad at a young age and that she had also recently lost her brother to lung cancer. I observed that there is a concern regarding the wife's understanding of her husband's poor condition and suggest that she talk again with the patient's physician's regarding his prognosis. The facility social worker expressed concerns that the wife is in denial.

That afternoon the physician holds a family conference with the patient and his family. The doctor advises the family that the patient's condition has worsened and he feels that if left on life support that the patient may still expire within days. Family seeks the guidance of their family pastor and consults in prayer regarding honoring the patient's wishes versus keeping him alive. His wife and family remains hopeful that the patient will improve and continue on against the direction of the physician and the patient's wishes and asks that life support be continued.

The following day the patient is uncommunicative. The family is very distraught and angry at the medical staff for allowing this to happen to their loved one. The hospice nurse offers another consultation visit, however family refuse. Family is observed standing over the patient and telling him not to leave them. The patient appears to be in terminal restlessness and is requiring medications for comfort, however his wife has asked that medications not be given to him in hopes that he will wake up. They are angry at staff and ask to see the doctor again to consider other options for treatment. The doctor tells the family that the patient may only have hours to live. The family hold out in hope that the doctor is wrong and the patient dies just as the doctor had said.

Concerns

In this scenario the patient had expressed his wishes for his end of life care. He had verbalized an acceptance of his mortality and had expressed preparation and readiness to die. Whereas his wife, feeling the emotional toll of loss and being left with the care of her family, financial burden and anticipatory grief, could not bear to lose the patriarch of the family. Denial kept her in a safe place of not accepting what she was being told. Other family responded as they knew how within their own coping mechanisms and with their lack of support, enabled the wife to fail to see that her spouses life was coming to a close.

Family were not afforded the opportunity of closure and being able to say goodbye. The children were not permitted to give acceptance to their dad and giving him permission to let go. No activities for memory making were offered and family was left angry and surprised at the sudden change of events.

In these instances there is concern as to if the patient was in conflict. I have seen patients who are at the point of transitioning from life to death and their family stand over the bed and tell them not to go and not to leave them. These patients are most often observed as restless and anxious. At times families find the courage to give permission and in succession the patient will calm down and pass peacefully.

Although fictional, these are the types of problems that are seen in hospice care and as the treating physician and hospice care would like to offer a patient a peaceful death, our hands are tied to offer any form of support or help.

Thankfully some hospice care facilities offer community bereavement support to families who have lost a loved one not admitted under their services. The second scenario, again fictional, presents a more satisfactory case. It shows a patient and family who have typically had prior exposure to the death of a loved one and have had some previous experience with hospice care.

Scenario # 2

Medical Assessment

Mrs. Jones is an 89 year old, white widowed, female, who is Catholic by faith. Mrs. Jones is a resident in long term care and has resided at her current facility for nine years. Mrs. Jones has diagnosis of end stage congestive heart failure. She has had multiple admissions to the hospital in the past 6 months, all related to her condition. Her physician has advised Mrs. Jones and her daughter Sheila that her condition has worsened and is recommending hospice care for comfort measures.

Social Work Assessment

Mrs. Jones had reported that her spouse died 5 years ago in hospice care and she has longed to be with him since his passing. She shared that she has lived a great life and due to her debilitating condition her quality of life is minimal. She said that she has developed close relationships with various facility staff and residents and after seeing multiple friends die, she feels that she is accepting of her diagnosis and prognosis. She has stated that she and her daughter have spoken openly about her death and that she has even went so far as to write out her own obituary. She said that she and her spouse made their funeral arrangements years ago. She said that it is so hard to wake up each day, knowing that she can no longer enjoy life as she once did. She said that she has prayed to God multiple times to take her and that she is "ready to go home".

Sheila has stated that being an only child makes the situation really difficult, however she is accepting and approving of her mom's wishes for end of life care. She said that they have taken the opportunity to openly talk with each other and share their love for one another. Sheila said that she has told her mom that she will be okay and not to worry about her.

The next day her condition exacerbates and she is admitted into the hospital. She is unresponsive and doctors feel that she may only have a few days to live. Hospice is consulted and the patient is admitted for comfort measures. Comfort medications for anxiety, pain and breathing are administered. Emotional and spiritual care support is provided by the hospice team. Closure issues have been provided by out of town family through phone closure and it appears that the patient and family are at peace. Family are tearful but coping appropriately. The patient dies later that evening with her daughter at her side. She expresses her gratitude for the care provided to her and her mom.

Concerns

No concerns are recognized in this situation. The patient was ready and her daughter was ready. The patient took on the responsibility of assuring that plans were in place to meet her needs and that her daughter understood her wishes. The patient died a good death. She was comfortable, at peace and ready to go. Her daughter had the support of her family and of both the hospital and hospice staff. She was at her mom's bedside when she died and although tearful was at peace.

It is apparent that these two scenarios are vastly different, however in reality there are people who come into the dying process with a readiness and acceptance. Perhaps it is their faith or the fact that they can no longer enjoy life. There are obviously many factors that influence a good or bad death and having information to help a family in their choices is my goal to avoiding a bad death.

Chapter 13

Protocol for Providing Dignity at the Time of Death

In the hospital and nursing home settings, dignity can be lost with the chaos and familiarity of everyday activity. Life goes on around us as though it is a normal day. Staff are laughing and other patients are in the halls. Alarms are going off in the background and it would seem that life should stop in the moments of our pain. Yet life continues without concern for our feelings or what terrible event just happened to us. It all seem so surreal. How can my loved one be gone?

Focusing in at the time just prior to death and assuring that patients and families have dignity is of upmost importance to me. Taking simple steps to assure privacy by closing a door, drawing a shade, asking visitors to knock or keeping room volume down, are ways that dignity can be granted.

Be aware of the thoughts and feelings of the patients and their families. Think from time to time about the experiences and the deep guttural expressions of grief and pain and where they are in the process of their loss. Think about their emotional state and remember in your own life your feelings of loss. Consider how you can provide some level of encouragement, help or support to your patients and families. Hospitals can be cold and callous, as the mundane activity becomes surreal.

Daily care of terminally ill patients create an insensitivity in staff and can result with the appearance of cold and detached workers, pressing aside from personal pain and tragedy. It is important as health care professionals to maintain compassion, while protecting oneself from overexposure to the heat of critical care.

Families become tired and grow hardened from the daily grind of care. It is easy to feel numb and at times unaware of your surroundings. Allowing others to help in your caregiving and giving assistance to suggest ideas about maintaining dignity might be of help to you. Below are some thoughts of consideration when working with patients and families during the dying process or at the time of death. As a visitor be aware of your interactions with patients in the dying process and with the need of their families.

Be Aware of Sights and Sounds

On many occasions I have found myself entering a patient's room where the TV is blaring and there is not a family member in sight. I look down and see that the patient is nonresponsive. I always question why the TV is on and why at times it is so loud. I have found patients where the door is shut or the TV is loud to seemingly mask the sound of moaning or rapid breathing. The patient appears to be deriving no benefits, so I will generally shut it off, unless the family says otherwise.

It seems that there are inevitable sounds such as the beeping and chirping of the medical machines that repeatedly alarm. I have noticed that some families have been shown by hospital staff how to silence the machines. However, there are those times when the floor RN is required to make it stop.

There is that moment in the intensive care unit, where the door is open and the patient's room is right next to the unit desk. The curtain is open and unit staff are speaking quite loudly in the hallway. Some ICU units appear to be constructed for privacy and noise reduction, where others are not afforded this same liberty. I strive to shut the door, draw the blinds and give the patient and family some level of dignity and privacy. Consider the following fictional scenario regarding patient dignity.

Scenario #1

One day while covering a hospice case there was a patient who was going to be weaned from life support. It appeared that the occurrence of ventilator weans was a common procedure that seemed to be too familiar to the staff on this hospital unit. The patient was extubated from life support and the nurse was in the room typing on the bedside computer. The door and the blinds to the hallway were open. There was a flurry of activity in the hallway and life proceeded like that of an assembly line; one vent wean in one room and another vent wean in the next.

Unit staff were going about their business with little regard to the family. Other family were walking by and peering into the room. The patient's family stood in the busy hallway in the flurry of activity, while waiting anxiously to say their goodbyes to their loved one. I stood at their side and felt very awkward for their discomfort. I found myself apologizing for the lack of control and activity around them.

I am not sure if the situation could have been different given the environment that the patient was in. It was my focus to shut the door, close the blinds, give the patient and family privacy and not hover. The nurse remained in the room, typing on the bedside computer, until the patient died. The family were very anxious and appeared uncomfortable with what was happening.

This scenario portrays a lack of dignity and compassion. Perhaps efforts could have been made to move the family to an empty room or outside of the unit. The staff could have set the room up with tissues, snacks and drinks and left the room to give the family time alone. There are many things that could have been done differently.

In my position I have the opportunity to visit multiple hospitals and one in particular represents the dignity model quite well. The rooms are large, private, and far apart from each other to provide a sense of separation. Staff facilitate the removal of life support as family step into the hallway, but because the area is so large it is not restrictive or congested. The room is set up with tissues and a snack cart with snacks and drinks for the family. There are chairs where family can sit. It is done very professionally and the patient and family are afforded dignity.

Reduce the Flurry of Visitor and Staff Activity

I can see that it is important to monitor staff activity and the purposefulness of coming in and out of the room. In most cases staff activity is more minimal, whereby family will report that they can't get the nurse or aide to come with a timely response. There may be other times when the staff is very present and very responsive to the needs of the patient.

As a health care provider, I like the idea of bedside charting, especially on a tablet device, for there is no clicking when using the screen method. It is quiet and would appear unobtrusive to the patient. In cases where there is no family present, family may find comfort with a hospice staff person sitting with the patient and doing paperwork. In other instances where families are present in the room, doing notes at bedside might be considered cold and may be better accomplished elsewhere outside of the room.

Many families will have the nurse post a sign on the door asking that visitors check in at the nurses' station before entering the patient's room. As health care professionals and family we have to remain sensitive to the needs of the patient and their immediate families. We do not want to draw from their strength.

I feel for families who find themselves repeating the events of the day over and over again to every person who calls or visits. This can be very draining on families. Instead I try and touch base with the caregiver and ask how I can be of assistance. I will check in on their coping and give them time to ventilate if needed. Sometimes I will offer to sit with the patient while they go smoke or get something to eat or go home and get a shower or let out their pets.

Reflect on the purpose of your visit and duration of your stay. Think about where the patient and family are at emotionally and ask yourself if the visit is for them or for yourself. Think about the limited time they have with their loved one and respect their wishes.

Be Aware of Light

Upon entering a room, observe if all of the lights in the room are on or if the window blinds are up. Notice if the sun is shining through the window, right into the face of the patient. There are patients whose family report that they loved the sun and the outdoors and don't appear at all phased that light is shining on the patient. Some people like to sleep with the lights on, whereas others may not. One common complaint that I hear from patients is how the nurse will come into their room in the middle of the night and turn on every light in the room. Remember to be sensitive to the needs of the patient in order to maintain dignity.

One day I went into a patient's room and the bed was turned around facing the window, looking outside. It was fairly bright in the room. The patient was alert and oriented and had family at the bedside. The patient had made an end of life decision for comfort care. This patient was a lover of the outdoors, boating, and fishing. The family explained that the patient loved the water and wanted to spend the last moments enjoying the outdoors. In this situation the patient was able to verbalize his wishes and supported a positive outcome as enjoying the sun one last time was the perfect medicine.

I have seen people in both the hospital and at home participate in this very thing. I have even been told of people who wanted to die outside. So it is important to consider the needs and wishes of the patient when considering light.

There are those times when the family may want it bright and the patient does not. It has been my observation that the window blinds may be fully open. It is of course always helpful to check in with the family to ask about their preference, while being sensitive to create a comfortable light temperature for the patient.

There also may be those times when entrance into a room may be dark because family are trying to catch up on some much needed sleep and there are those other families who just like to sit in the dark. I have noticed that some older people have a light sensitivity and cannot handle bright lights. So be aware of the light needs of the patient.

Ensure a Presence of Peace and Calm

It is our job to educate families about the dying process, patient comfort and creating an atmosphere of patient peace. It is amazing how unresponsive patients can react to the presence of their families through either calm quiet breathing or with restlessness.

Unfortunately some families can be insensitive to the behaviors around their sick loved one. Keep in mind the family and what is normal for them may not be normal for you. Some families are very jovial and talk openly in front of the patient. Others are very quiet and move all conversation to the hallway. Some are loud and stand over the patient talking to them telling them not to leave and to wake up.

It can be difficult to watch as a family in denial creates a hovering conflicting situation for the patient. At the same time, it can be hard to respect the wishes of the family and maintain some level of serenity for the dying patient. Be aware of your own issues which can cause feelings of discomfort if things are out of the norm for you. Education is a helpful tool that can be used to ensure that family are aware of how to treat a dying patient with comfort and dignity.

Some families that I have noticed are very sensitive to the patient being at peace and will play soft music or have artificial candle light as a way of maintaining a calm comfortable atmosphere.

Whatever the norm is for the family, education regarding creating a place of calm for the patient may be helpful if the patient is experiencing anxiety or restlessness.

Restrict Conversation to the Family

Be sensitive about your conversation and attempt to keep focus on the patient and family. Try not to spend time talking about yourself and your problems. I have found that there are those times when it is helpful to share stories or experiences of other patients or families as a generalization to help family with their coping or for educational purposes. Yet I have to be aware if I am taking precious time away from a family, which should be spent between the patient and the family.

When my father-in-law died he was at home and had a hospice continuous care nurse at his bedside. His nurse took it upon herself to fill in all quiet time with stories of herself, her illnesses, her family, her family's business, where she lived, grew up, etc. This went on for hours until the final moments when she was asked to leave the room. This caregiver had no ill intent in continuous talking, but it took from the intimacy of the family and their time with their patriarch.

This experience helps me to be sensitive to what I am talking about and the length of my conversations.

Give Family Some Space and Privacy

There are times when a family member may ask a staff person to stay with them, but there are times when our hovering is not a comfort. There are those times when I go to see a patient and the family member designated as security guard blocks the door or asks to meet with me in the hallway. Nurses of course have to assess the patient by observation and upon educating family they will typically allow entry. Be sensitive to the family's request for privacy. Be aware of your time with the patient and the family and the purposes of your stay. It is amazing how after dealing with families you can tell those who are inviting and those who can't give enough hints for you to exit the room.

I have witnessed that many hospice staff nurses check in with family periodically over the course of the day and make themselves available to family by phone. This seems to be a very productive application to supporting privacy and space.

Support the Family

Be present for the needs of the family. Inquire as to family coping and closure support needs. Ask the family how you may be of assistance and let experience be your guide regarding your interactions.

During ventilator weans, I have seen some hospital staff set up the room. They ensure that there are tissues in place, chairs, water and even at some facilities, they will bring in a snack tray with drinks, snacks, and fruit. Some hospitals give the patient a blanket or have a person in place so that the patient does not die alone. On occasion families will bring in a CD player and keep music playing. Think about how the patient and family can both be comforted.

Children may need to participate in some form of closure activity to make a memory of their loved one such as: finger prints, tracing there loved one's hand or drawing pictures. Some children may find it helpful to create a collage of old photographs.

Inquire as to how it is that you can be of assistance to the needs of the family. Ask yourself how you can be of help, to ease their pain and suffering.

Spiritual Care

Ask if the patient or family has any spiritual care needs. Is there a need for a priest, rabbi, an imam or a chaplain? Does the family need prayer or assistance for a spiritual concern? Are there any specific rites or rituals that the patient requires? Can the patient and family benefit from group prayer? I have seen some groups pray around the patient and also sing over the patient. Be aware that spiritual care needs sometimes will help the patient pass.

I have been with families who will request a priest or pastor for end of life prayer. The prayer will be offered and within minutes the patient will die. So spiritual care can be very important to the patient and family in the dying process.

Timely Weans

As a health care professional who works in the hospice field it is very important to make sure that the hospice team has done their part to ensure that weans occur as planned. This is a way to lessen the worry and meet the expectations of the family. Experiencing delays and creating greater frustration and stress do not make for a peaceful death. There will be times when things just don't fall into place, but strive to ensure that things do.

Be Aware of Your Grief Reactions

Be aware of your own triggers and times of discomfort. Utilize the strengths of others to ensure that the patient and the family have their needs met. Be sensitive to your own grief reactions and previous experiences that could create conflict when working with a patient, family, or hospital staff person. Be aware of internal feelings and the emotional withdraw being made from your reserves of strength. If you are a faith filled person, create a sense of control through prayer for divine help before entering into a chaotic or crisis centered situation. Ensure that you have eaten before extending yourself, knowing that it will take significant concentration and emotional effort to be present for the patient and family. Monitor your use of the telephone and silence calls.

Be Aware of the Needs of the Hospital Staff

Take into consideration that staff may he having a busy or emotional day. Be aware that staff may be experiencing triggers and concerns regarding the patient and their experiences with death and dying. Focus on the needs of the staff and ask how you can help to assist in coordination of effective and timely patient care. Express your gratitude for staff assistance.

Chapter 14

Making Memories

The process of making memories for future generations is a process whereby patients and families can take part in creating memories together. There are those times where families may not want to acknowledge that their loved one is dying and feel that participating in such an activity is not necessary. However, thinking about ideas ahead of time may strike more of an urgency if the patient's condition falls into a rapid decline.

My own family did a few video recordings of my loved one telling stories from his past. In hind sight my wife shared that she wished that she had recorded more of his stories. I had mentioned earlier writing a letter of thankfulness to my parents. I have heard of patients writing a letter in advance for their children to read later in life.

The nice thing about making memories is there are no right or wrong options. There are plenty of ideas on the internet and with the available internet search sites, it would be easy to come up with an idea. However, for those who may lack creativity, some things that we offer families in hospice care include making a hand print or finger print of the patient and either putting in on a piece of paper or flower pot. I have seen some people who have done this on canvas and with each family member adding their hand print it makes for a nice piece of art when framed.

Other ideas include making a cast mold with plaster of the patient and their loved one holding hands. There are kits available online. Another suggestion is photography or video. Children may like to participate in tracing their loved one's hand and coloring in the picture. The child can then put their hand in the middle of their loved ones hand. Some people plant trees or flowers together. Again whatever you decide, so long as you do it together, helps to create an eternal connection, so when your family member dies, there is something to remember your loved one by.

I have heard of teddy bears being made out of the patient's blanket or a piece of their favorite clothing item. Some people will add the material to a pillow case. I have seen t-shirts and quilts made to honor loved ones. Be creative and enjoy your time with your loved one.

Chapter 15

Near Death Awareness

Near death awareness involves situations whereby patients will express an awareness of transitioning and may verbalize speaking with deceased loved ones.

It is common to hear stories of patients who say that they see Jesus or that they have talked with a deceased loved one. In my work at hospice care, I have found that often times patients are reluctant to tell their family this information for fear that they will think they are crazy. Yet when I am with families I will probe and ask if their loved ones have talked about seeing any deceased family members or cried out to someone in the room and more than not, families will answer yes.

Interestingly enough I have had people tell me about situations where they died and were hovering over their body looking down at the room. But more often family will say that their loved one was talking to a family member who died years prior. I can recall one woman who was talking to her brother who had died 40 years ago. It is the strangest thing at times, when standing beside a patient in their room, as they stare up at the ceiling or look off into the corner of the room.

Other times I have noticed that the person will be tracking something or someone in the room with their eyes, yet not conscious that I am standing right in front of them. Many feel that the patient is hallucinating or delusional from changes from medication or physiological changes.

I can remember on various occasions having patients who would be unconscious for days and suddenly wake up and start talking with their family. I had a personal experience with a family member who in the week prior to his death experienced a similar episode. He was extremely confused and fearful one day, and the next, as though it had never happened, he was alert and oriented. He reported that he had been away and was not sure how to get back to his family. He was overflowing with love and affection for his family and could not express his love deep enough.

I recall other situations where this similar type of event happened. One woman looked as though she had been in heaven. She had been unconscious for days and when I walked into her room she had an aura around her like she was glowing with love. She could not stop telling her family how much she loved them. Closure occurred between the patient and her family and following this event she died shortly afterwards.

This type of experience does not happen all of the time. However there are many patient cases when the patient will go through a rally right before they die. Family will admit their loved one into hospice care thinking that they are going to pass and the next day, the patient will rally. The patient will be able to talk and laugh and respond to their family as though they are getting better, when in reality it is just a rally before they pass. Family will second guess themselves and think it is a miracle, when it fact it is a gift to say goodbye. These events often are confusing to families, however with education, families can prepare should this happen.

I believe that God allows patients to say goodbye to their family and to allow them the opportunity to express their love and in turn receive their love from their family.

I had a family member share a story on the day of his rally that was so vivid and so real, he continued to share it over and over again. He said that he knew he was away and could not get back to his family. In the midst of his fearful situation he cried out to the Lord and said instantly he was free. This experience helped him be comforted by his faith in God and the support of his family.

Another time I had a patient in the nursing home after being unresponsive for days, woke up and asked for something to eat, like nothing had ever happened. The process of dying is truly a mystery and as a hospice worker I have had the privilege of being an observer of patients who experience near death awareness.

Our loved ones tell us what they want, yet at times we ignore their requests because we do not want to accept that their lives are coming to a close. Listening to patients share of near death awareness whereby they share of seeing family who has passed on or angels or Jesus helps us to tune into the patient and the preparation for their passing. Sometimes patients may start to talk about these things months before their passing. Should your loved one talk about these types of experiences, be gentle and reassuring, giving heed to what they have to say. Try not to persuade that what they experienced was not real.

One day I was in the hospital as a patient and another patient was sitting with me waiting on a stress test. The man shared that he had a heart attack months ago and while in the emergency room his chest felt as though an elephant was sitting on him. He said that all of the sudden he was out of his body looking down at the staff working on him. He said that the next thing he was in this white sphere and his pain was completely gone. He said that he felt so loved and so much peace, that he did not want to come back. He said that all of the sudden he heard the doctors say that they were losing him. He said that they put the paddles to his heart and the next thing he was back in his body and the pain was again unbearable. He said that having had this experience, eliminated his fear of death.

Another patient who I had worked with had an end stage condition which required her to have frequent visits to the hospital. One day she went to the hospital and while there she said that she saw Jesus out her window. She said that this experience gave her great peace and comfort and that she was no longer afraid to die. I can see that God had prepared her for her death which occurred some months later.

I have noticed many people who have these experiences say that they have a peace that comes and remains with them until they pass. They will disclose that these experiences help eliminate their fear of death or confirm their faith in God. It is interesting in other reading material about after life experiences where stories will be told of heaven and how a crowd of loved ones will come to greet the person.

It is important to listen to the patient and without fear ask if they have experienced these near death awareness situations. Listen with an open mind and be supportive. If they have had these experiences try not to be alarmed, but keep in mind that perhaps they are being prepared for their passing.

Chapter 16

Pets

Who loves us more than our pets? On my desk at work I have a photograph of a terminally ill patient who, lying in bed, has his golden retriever lying right up on the bed with him. He is embracing and loving his dog. Thank God that He gives us the unconditional love of our animals. I have heard of countless stories of patients and their love for their animals. I have worked in hospice care in the nursing home setting and have always been amazed at how animals will lift the sad countenance of patients.

It triggers a story of a horse name Pistol Pete. I was filled with joy myself the first time I met him and the lady who brought him around to the nursing homes. He was a miniature horse, standing about four feet tall. On his back he had a saddle with a stuffed bear riding on him and on his feet, children's light up tennis shoes. He had a long mane and big dark eyes with long eye lashes. He had a cowboy hat on his head. He appeared to have great patience as his very appearance would bring light and happiness to all who visited with him. Residents would chuckle and want to talk and pet him. I myself couldn't take my eyes off of this little guy. He was so cute. He lived a life of serving others and brought such great joy to the life of those nursing home residents.

A nurse that I worked with had a dog by the name of Sugar. Sugar was a trained volunteer dog and would visit the patients at one of the facilities we covered. I remember this one day we had a patient who did not speak English and was very stoic and almost stone like. My friend put Sugar on her lap and for the first time we stood amazed as this patient smiled and lifted her frail hand to pet Sugar. The event nearly brought us both to tears.

I have heard of stories of pets' devotion to their owners in which a patient's cat or dog senses that death is near and will remain with their owner until the time of their passing, disregarding their own comfort needs over the needs of their owner.

I have watched as patients filled with pain and anxiety overflow with joy and love the moment their dog would step foot into their room. Animals of all types bring about the innocence of life, of unconditional love, and acceptance. They don't care if you have bad breath, you're sick, or if you don't feel well. They keep our secrets and don't tell our tales. They are truly God's gifts to humans and are a vital part of patient and family closure.

Being that I am an animal lover, I always try to ensure that patients have contact with their animals. Sometimes circumstances do not allow a patient to see their animal before they die, but some hospitals will make allowances. Our hospice units allow animal visitors, so keep in mind of your location and ask if your loved one can receive a visit from their pet.

Consider the importance and value of helping your family member have the opportunity to say goodbye to their pet. For many patients their pets are like children and being able to talk with their pets and say goodbye should be supported.

Chapter 17

Conclusion

We have taken the walk of experiencing the dying process and concern that patients and family have as they make this transition. The journey often creates a range of emotions and feelings which leaves patients and families feeling bewildered and fearful about the future. Barriers to accessing end of life support and accepting hospice care originate from individual aspects of personality and coping mechanisms.

Accepting hospice support allows for an interdisciplinary and holistic approach to ensuring that the patient and family needs are met. As patients and families move forward in physical decline an adjustment period occurs, whereby progressive steps are made towards ensuring aspects of closure.

Looking at ourselves and our coping mechanisms helps us to be more insightful of our patient and family needs. It helps to recognize the need for self-care and supporting an ideology that will overflow to those of whom we care for.

The motion of moving into the dying process, helps create reflection and supports personal growth as we pay closer attention to how we communicate our love to our families.

Families can utilize tools such as journaling to help them cope in more effective ways. Avenues of making memories and honoring our loved ones with memory gardens and various other memorabilia enriches the death experience and makes our grief less crushing.

Finally, being cognizant of ways in which we can help our loved ones have a peaceful, compassionate, and comfortable death will create in us a sense of satisfaction and achievement knowing that we were able to honor our loved one and ensure that everything was done to help in his dignity and transition.

I want to extend my thanks for your taking time to read this book and learn about the dying process. It is my hope that you will find this information a valuable resource to be used when

143

either dealing with a family member or coming to the aid of friend or a patient. Thank you and God Bless!

Please feel free to complete a book review of this title and leave your comments regarding the information at the website from which it was purchased Thank you!

Made in the USA
Monee, IL
28 September 2020